Ho'oponopono

Advanced Ho'oponopono Secrets

©2018 Colin G Smith

http://AwesomeMindSecrets.com

Disclaimer

This eBook is for educational purposes only, and is not intended to be a substitute for professional counselling, therapy or medical treatment. Nothing in this eBook is intended to diagnose or treat any pathology or diseased condition of the mind or body. The author will not be held responsible for any results of reading or applying the information.

Table of Contents

About The Author 1

Introduction 2

Spirituality 13

Relationships 21

Money & Finances 28

Health & Wellbeing 31

Other Cool Tools 35

Appendix 38

Further Reading 40

Websites 41

About The Author

For over fifteen years now I have been driven to find the very best methods of personal transformation and secrets to beneficially and magically altering our perception of reality. If you are anything like me, you're probably interested in simple and straight-forward explanations. Practical stuff that gets results! I am a NLP Master Practitioner, writer & author who has written several books including:

- Love Yourself Lovable: Realising Your Authentic Loving Self Through The Profound Yet Simple Practice Of Ho'oponopono
- The NLP ToolBox: Your Guide Book to Neuro Linguistic Programming NLP Techniques
- Thought Symbols Magick: Manifest Your Desires in Life using the Secret Power of Sigil Magic and Thought Forms

Introduction

"Ho'oponopono is a profound gift that allows one to develop a working relationship with the Divinity within and learn to ask that in each moment, our errors in thought, word, deed, or action be cleansed. **The process is essentially about freedom, complete freedom from the past.***"* - Morrnah Nalamaku Simeona

In this guidebook you will discover advanced Ho'oponopono techniques for improving all areas of your life. I will keep this introduction chapter brief because I covered the basics in my previous book, *"Ho'oponopono: Healing Your Life With The Ancient Hawaiian Secret Power-Prayer Practice of Love And Forgiveness."*

Inside these pages I will reveal to you many wonderful advanced Ho'oponopono secrets that will enhance your practice, including the following gems:

- **Ho'oponopono Tibetan Style:** This is a special breathing meditation that helps you transform negativity while increasing your courage, love and compassion.

- **Inner Child Meditation:** Discover how to connect to your inner child allowing you to develop a loving relationship with this part of yourself leading to an increased sense of wellbeing.

- **Higher Self Meditation:** Connect with your own Higher Self or Soul which will give you a greater sense of connection with your own source of pure unconditional love, peace and wisdom.

- **Ho'oponopono Higher Self / Inner Child Healing Process:** This is a very powerful process that enables you to align your *inner family* in a way that allows for harmonious healing and transformation of *erroneous data* stored in your *inner child* or Lower Self.

- **Ideal Partner Manifestation:** If you would like help from the Universe to find your ideal partner, this special prayer ritual can help you. It utilises the power of Blessing, combined with the energetic connections we have with other people in the word.

- **Relationship Shadows Into De-Light:** This process enables you to bring your own shadow aspects to light, transmute them with Ho'oponopono, while developing more empathy and compassion for yourself and other people. It can be surprising what's revealed with this powerful technique.

- **Ho'oponopono Magic In A Bottle:** Enjoy preforming *random acts of kindness* with this fun method that will bless complete strangers while introducing them to Ho'oponopono.

- **Wrathful Ho'oponopono:** Discover how to practice Ho'oponopono even when you are really angry and upset with someone. You can use the magical mantra and transmute your anger into a peaceful state of calm instead.

Along with those described above, you'll find many more advanced Ho'oponopono techniques inside this guidebook which are categorised under the following chapters: Spirituality, Relationships, Money & Finances, Health & Wellbeing and Other Cool Tools. So if you have a pressing problem you would like to solve, discover a relevant tool or two by browsing through the appropriate category. To start off though, let's look at the most important part of Ho'oponopono...

Your Authentic Self: Pure Unconditional Love

"The PURPOSE of life is to be RESTORED BACK to LOVE, Moment by Moment." To fulfill this purpose, the individual must acknowledge that he is 100 PERCENT RESPONSIBLE for creating his life the way it is. He must come to see that it is his thoughts that create his life the way it is moment to moment. The problems are not people, places and situations but rather THE THOUGHTS OF THEM. He must come to appreciate that there is no such thing as 'out there.'" - Dr. Hew Len

Ho'oponopono has it's roots going back into traditional Hawaiian history, where it was performed as a family healing ceremony held by a priest or wise elder. However towards the end of the twentieth century, renowned Hawaiian Kahuna Healer, Morrnah Simeona, realised that a new form of Ho'oponopono was needed in order to help modern day people derive benefit from it. In her new method known as, *Self Identity Through Ho'oponopono*, which is what most people now know of as simply, *"Ho'oponopono,"* the transformation happens between the person and Divinity. To transmute problems, a person directs the following sentences to Divinity: *"I love you / I'm sorry / Please forgive me / Thank you."* It doesn't matter in what order these sentences are said, as long as they are repeated over and over again like reciting a mantra. By doing so, we can surrender to the divine source of unconditional love, let go of our intellectual ego grasping, and allow Divinity to transmute our problems instead - leading to more peace and freedom.

Modern day Ho'oponopono is essentially about solving problems by cleaning, clearing or deleting the *erroneous data* that is stored in our subconscious *database*. Doing the practice helps us achieve this while connecting more deeply with our authentic loving self. And that is the main purpose of Ho'oponopono: To realise our authentic self identity - **Pure Unconditional Love**.

Almost Dead With Thirst

Shibli was asked: "Who guided you in the path?"

Shibli said: "A dog. One day I saw him, almost dead with thirst, standing by the water's edge. Every time he looked at his reflection in the water he was frightened and withdrew, because he thought it was another dog."

"Finally, such was his necessity, he cast away fear and leapt into the water; at which the reflection disappeared."

"The dog found that the obstacle, which was himself, the barrier between him and what he sought, melted away."

"In this same way, my own obstacle vanished when I knew that it was what I took to be my own self. And my way was first shown to me by the behaviour of... a dog."

"You bark, you fight, you fall in love, you make friends and enemies, and every person is functioning like a mirror to you. It has to be so! Unless you awake, and unless you <u>realise who you are</u>, you will continue seeing in the mirrors of others your own reflection - making love to your own reflection, fighting with your own reflection." - Osho (Journey To The Heart: Discourses On The Sufi Way)

So, again, it's well worth repeating, the main purpose of modern day Ho'oponopono is to realise our authentic self identity; pure unconditional love. One of the best things we can do to improve our life is to stop dwelling on ego-based *data* and practice surrendering to the Divine source within ourselves to solve all our problems. A useful analogy is to imagine a pure, clean white board with a letter 'M' in the middle. The 'M' represents memories or *data*; the memories, beliefs and *programs* that continuously arise from the collective subconscious *database*. None of it is who we really are but we get tricked into identifying with it and this *data* can cause us real problems such as feelings of anxiety, anger and despair. But the good news is that with practice we can learn how to switch our identification back to our authentic loving self. The 90 Second Rule can help us remember how simple this can be:

The 90 Second Rule

"When a person has a reaction to something in their environment, there's a 90 second chemical process that happens in the body; after that, any remaining emotional response is just the person choosing to stay in that emotional loop. Something happens in the external world and chemicals are flushed through your body which puts it on full alert. For those chemicals to totally flush out of the body it takes less than 90 seconds. This means that for 90 seconds you can watch the process happening, you can feel it happening, and then you can watch it go away. After that, if you continue to feel fear, anger, and so on, you need to look at the thoughts that you're thinking that are re-stimulating the circuitry that is resulting in you having this physiological response over and over again." - Dr. Jill Bolte Taylor (Neuroanatomist and author of, *"My Stroke of Insight"*)

To summarise, if you find yourself in negative states of consciousness (which is due to the erroneous *data* arising in your subconscious mind), start repeating the Ho'oponopno mantra, remembering your own Divine Source as you do so, and within 90 seconds you'll find yourself in a much better state of being.

The Ho'oponopono Principles

The following set of principles form the ethos of Ho'oponopono practice. At first glance they could appear to be simplistic but they are in fact based on profound spiritual understanding. The more you practice Ho'oponopono and become familiar with these as living principles, the more you will come to appreciate the profound benefits they provide. So let's take a look at the principles now:

I Don't Know, So Let Go!

"Truth cannot be said. And all that can be said will not be true." - Lao Tzu

We like to think we understand what is happening but the fact is people, situations, life is far to complex; we don't really have a clue what is going on moment to moment! There is an immense amount of information filtered through our senses and then that information is filtered again through our belief systems. Our ego likes to trick us into believing our arrogant assumptions and judgements but if we're honest, most of the time we are in, *"the deep sleep of ignorance,"* as Buddha put it.

The great thing about living the, *"I Don't Know, So Let Go!,"* principle though is that it helps us to let go, relax and surrender to the Divine source. By practicing this principle we can learn to step back from our assumptions and judgements, and acknowledge that, *"I don't really know what is happening. Only the Divine really knows what is going on so I might as well, relax, let go of my intellectual ego-grasping and surrender to Divinity by practicing Ho'oponopono."*

I Can't Control Reality

"The intellect working alone can't solve these problems, because the intellect only manages. Managing things is no way to solve problems. You want to let them go! When you do Ho'oponopono, what happens is that the Divinity takes the painful thought and neutralizes or purifies it. You don't purify the person, place, or thing. You neutralize the energy you associate with that person, place, or thing. So the first stage of Ho'oponopono is the purification of that energy.

"Now something wonderful happens. Not only does that energy get neutralized; it also, gets released, so there's a brand-new slate. Buddhists call it the Void. The final step is that you allow the Divinity to come in and fill the void with light.

"To do Ho'oponopono, you don't have to know what the problem or error is. All you have to do is notice any problem you are experiencing physically, mentally, emotionally, whatever. Once you notice, your responsibility is to immediately begin to clean, to say, 'I'm sorry. Please forgive me.'" - Dr. Hew Len

If we don't really know what is happening in reality, we can't be in control of it. Again, our ego likes to trick us into thinking we can control reality or bend it to our will but really we have no control; reality is far to vast and complex. One of the main powers we have as human beings is the ability to make choices. The thing is most of the time these decisions are influenced by erroneous *data* in our subconscious minds.

With Ho'oponopono we begin to realise that the best choice we can make is to *clean data* while surrendering to Divinity to solve our problems and provide us with inspiration. *This is an approach to living that can be called, *surrender*; it's about letting go of trying to control everything and surrendering to Divinity.

*You can read more about this in the section titled, *"The 4 Stages of Awakening,"* in the Appendix.

Total Responsibility or 100% Responsibility

Ho'oponopono teaches us that to transform our lives and become more loving, we need to take **Total Responsibility** and practice transforming the problems that appear to us. The idea is that whatever we perceive or experience in our Universe, we take responsibility for it appearing to us; the understanding is that there is something within ourselves (erroneous subconscious *data*) that co-creates our experience of reality. More often than not, we try to push problems away in a state of non-acceptance, but unfortunately this approach tends to get poor results, like the old adage says, *"resistance causes persistence."* Total Responsibility is not about guilt though; it's about <u>acknowledging and accepting</u> that you have erroneous *data* within your subconscious mind that you begin to *clean* and *clear*.

We are connected to everyone and everything in the entire Universe. Our interactions and interconnectedness go back to *beginningless time*, so basically we really have no idea why problems appear to us in the here and now; the web of causes and effects is vast beyond comprehension. The following healing prayer that Morrnah Nalamaku Simeona used to recite sometimes before practicing Ho'oponopono encapsulates this understanding of interconnectedness:

"Divine creator, father, mother, son as one. If I, my family, relatives, and ancestors have offended you, your family, relatives, and ancestors in thoughts, words, deeds, and actions from the beginning of our creation to the present, we ask your forgiveness. Let this cleanse, purify, release, cut all the negative memories, blocks, energies, and vibrations and transmute these unwanted energies to pure light. And it is done."

The concept of Total Responsibility goes beyond what *you* say, do, and think; it even includes what *others* say, do, and think! Yes it's quite radical. Taking on this special point of view, means we stop blaming anyone or anything for our current experience of reality. It's not your fault but it is your responsibility to accept the problems you're presented with and transform them through proven transmutation methods such as Ho'oponopono.

Taking Total Responsibility for everything that appears in your Universe is a tall order but it's also really empowering. It means you can't blame anyone or anything for undesirable circumstances, and it places you in control of your own thoughts, feelings and perceptions. Total Responsibility is best experienced as being part of a daily spiritual practice that you have to continually remind yourself of because it's so antithesis to conventional societies, *"culture of blame."*

I've personally found it takes a lot of effort to adopt this mind-set, even after many months of daily practice; the inner child will shout and scream in an attempt to shirk responsibility. But when I do, I feel much more congruent within myself as an adult human being and it feels empowering.

Transmutation By Surrendering To Divinity

We can transmute any problem that appears in our Universe by surrendering to Divinity through the practice of Ho'oponopono. The problems that we experience are really just down to the erroneous memories or *data* stored in our subconscious mind. By *cleaning* this *data* we can let it go into the void or zero point and allow the Divine source to replace it with loving light instead. And because we don't really know what the problem or error is, we need to practice letting go and allow Divinity to solve our problem's using Divine wisdom and timing. Our task is to simply take responsibility and do the *cleaning*...

I Remember My Authentic Loving Self

"Ho'oponopono, a process of repentance, forgiveness, and transmutation, is a petition to Love to void and replace toxic energies with it's self. Love accomplishes this by flowing through the mind, beginning with the spiritual mind, the superconscious. It then continues it's flow through the intellectual mind, the conscious mind, freeing it of thinking energies. Finally, it moves into the emotional mind, the subconscious, voiding thoughts of toxic emotions and filling them with it's self." - Dr. Hew Len

Practice remembering your authentic loving self as much as possible. All the problems we experience are because of erroneous *data* stored in the subconscious *database*. None of this is who we really are but our ego get's tricked into identifying with it. The *data* is like the waves on the ocean, our authentic self is like the deepest depths of the ocean. The good news is, the more your practice Ho'oponopono, the more you realise your authentic loving self because that is the main purpose of the practice anyway.

"Our illusion of separation from Love is the root of all our suffering." - DeNoyelles

Pocket Principles

- I Don't Know, So Let Go!
- I Can't Control Reality
- Total Responsibility or 100% Responsibility
- Transmutation By Surrendering To Divinity
- I Remember My Authentic Loving Self

It's highly recommended that you write the Ho'oponopono principles down a piece of paper and carry it around in your pocket. Simply use a sheet of paper, folded four times: Write the principles down on one quadrant and on another quadrant you can write a letter 'M' in the middle, representing memories or *data*, and your authentic self is represented by the pure, clean, empty space. You can then read through the list on a regular basis throughout your day and contemplate these powerful principles. If you do this everyday for a few weeks these life-changing principles will become an habitual empowering mind-set.

Spirituality

Ho'oponopono Tibetan Style!

"By harnessing our breath for virtuous purposes we purify our inner winds, and when pure winds are flowing through our channels pure minds arise naturally." - Geshe Kelsang Gyatso - Eight Steps to Happiness

In Tibetan Buddhism there is a special breathing meditation healing practice known as Tonglen; this word means, *"taking and giving."* Tonglen meditation enables a person to TAKE in the *negative* aspects or energies of life, transform this energy into a useful purpose (e.g. cleaning *data*) and then GIVE OUT positive energy. This is a very powerful practice for transforming your problems and it helps you develop courage, love and compassion. It is of course made even more powerful by incorporating Ho'oponopono. Read through the instructions below and then give it a go...

Ho'oponopono Tonglen Meditation in 3 Steps

1. TAKING: Begin by representing your problem as black smoke. Simply imagine, sense or pretend that there is a cloud of black smoke in front of you. Say, *"I'm sorry,"* and begin to inhale this cloud of black smoke through your nostrils. Imagine the smoke entering into your body and settling at the area of your heart chakra. Pause your breath there for a moment and say, *"Please forgive me,"* as you allow that energy to dissolve the *erroneous ego data* held in your subconscious.

2. GIVING: Now slowly and gently exhale pure white wisdom light through your mouth saying the phrase, *"I love you,"* as you do so. You could if you wish imagine beautiful rays of white light and nectars radiating from your body. You are giving away all that is pure, coming from deep within your continually residing authentic loving self that is connected to the infinite source of pure unconditional love. As you exhale imagine that the white wisdom light is blessing every living being, bestowing peace and happiness!

3. REJOICING: As you're exhaling allow yourself to feel joy at practicing giving peace and happiness to others. Pause for a moment at the end of the breath and indulge in it! Say, *"Thank you."*

REPEAT: You now simply go back and start the taking & giving cycle again.

*Note: In Step 1 you represent any problem you want to transform as black smoke. You can also do this practice for other people, keeping in mind the 100% Responsibility principle, knowing that we are really just cleaning *data* within ourselves.

Inner Child Meditation

The Lower Self is responsible for generating our emotions and body sensations and we can also refer to this part as our *Inner Child*. All of the subconscious memories (*data*) from this life and previous lives are stored in this part of ourself. And it goes much deeper than that: We are also connected into a **collective** storehouse of memories.

We can discover more about our inner child aspects by becoming attentive to our emotional states and body feelings. The following exercise will help you learn how to become more aware of this part of yourself:

Welcoming Your Inner Child

1. Think about a situation that has triggered a painful reaction in you; maybe it was an interaction with a certain person.

See what you saw and hear what you heard in the situation. Relive it as vividly as possible.

Now become aware of your body feelings; notice where in your body those unpleasant feelings are located.

2. Now allow yourself to become aware of a childhood memory associated with this feeling; where in your past does that feeling originate from? Simply let your feelings guide you to the memory.

3. Notice that part of yourself: What does that inner child look like? Approximately how old do they look? As you become more aware of your inner child, you can feel yourself connecting more with that younger human being. Say, *"Hello,"* and maybe gently place your arm on their shoulder.

*Note: You can also look at photograph of your younger self if you find that helps you establish a better connection with your inner child.

Connecting with Your Higher Self

Your Higher Self / Soul / Super-Consciousness is the part of you that is immortal and connected to the source of unconditional love. We're always connected but with conscious effort in meditation we can become more aware of our connection and experience the flow of unconditional love more profoundly.

1. Close your eyes and imagine there is a golden sun or orb above your head.

2. Allow the light and energy from this Higher Self / Soul / Super-Consciousness to fill your whole being, right down to your toes.

3. Bathe yourself in this golden glowing, unconditional, loving energy. Enjoy this experience for at least 10 minutes.

With familiarity and practice you will become more aware of this incredible part of yourself; *your authentic loving self.* Persist with this meditation and simple visualisation every day and you will strengthen your connection with your Higher Self. With practice, you will be able to walk around outside of meditation, do the visualisation with your eyes open, and stay connected to the source of unconditional love and this will feel very empowering.

Ho'oponopono Higher Self / Inner Child Healing Process

1. Sit down somewhere comfortable; sitting outside in nature is always good if it's appropriate.

2. Close your eyes, relax and go within yourself.

3. Start repeating the Ho'oponopono mantra to yourself:

"I Love You"

"I'm Sorry"

"Please Forgive Me"

"Thank You"

4. Connecting with Your Higher Self:

As you keep on repeating the Ho'oponopono mantra, start imagining a golden sun or orb above your head.

Allow the light and energy from this Higher Self to fill your whole being, right down to your toes.

Bathe yourself in this golden glowing, unconditional, loving energy.

5. When you've started to feel empowered by this loving connection with your *parental guardian spirit* or Higher Self you can begin to allow yourself to discover the Inner Child memory that is causing you pain and discomfort.

6. Think about the situation that has triggered a painful reaction in you; maybe it was an interaction with a certain person:

See what you saw and hear what you heard in the situation. Relive it as vividly as possible.

Now become aware of your body feelings; notice where in your body those unpleasant feelings are located.

7. Now allow yourself to become aware of a childhood memory associated with this feeling; where in your past does that feeling originate from? Simply let your feelings guide you to the memory.

8. Notice that aspect of you; what does that inner child look like? About how old do they look? As you become more aware of your inner child, you can feel yourself connecting more with that younger human being.

9. Say hello to that younger self: Look into his/her eyes and say, *"Hi, I am you from the future. I have come to help you."* Maybe imagine putting your hand on their shoulder to reassure them. Now say, *"I'm so sorry you are suffering. I'm sorry you are experiencing pain. And I'm really sorry that up until now I haven't supported you well. Please forgive me. I love you. Thank you."* NOTE: You might have to communicate this a few times to make the connection with your inner child.

10. Now ask, *"Would you let me help heal your pain?"* (You'll probably get a positive response. If not go back to Step 9 and repeat that process.)

11. Re-connect with your Higher Self: Imagine the glowing sun/globe above your head bathing loving, healing golden light into your whole being. As you do that start repeating the Ho'oponopono mantra;

"I Love You"

"I'm Sorry"

"Please Forgive Me"

"Thank You"

12. While connected to your Higher Self and seeing your inner child, keep repeating the mantra for a while. NOTE: This could be just a couple of minutes or possibly 20 minutes. Practice will help you learn how to gauge the amount of time needed in each sitting. And remember this process is not a quick-fix solution; it's a process you can revisit again to continue healing your inner-child aspects.

Meditating On The Qualities Of Divine Love

This is a very simple meditation that can be surprisingly rewarding.

1. Sit down, close your eyes and begin to think about the qualities of Divine Love: Pure unconditional love, perfect peace, omniscient wisdom, pure bliss, divine void, perfect stillness, radiant loving presence and so on.

2. As you contemplate these Divine qualities begin to repeat the mantra, *"I love you," "thank you."*

Meditating With Mala Beads (Prayer Beads)

A useful way to get used to repeating mantra's over and over is with the help of mala beads. They can be made from seeds, wood, bone or gem stones and they look like necklaces or bracelets. You can sit and start reciting the Ho'oponopono mantra and count a bead for each round or count a bead for each line of the mantra if you prefer.

Mindful Walking

Another great thing about Ho'oponopono is that you can walk around while repeating the mantra. This can be a beautiful exercise to do outside in nature and the fresh air. There are various ways you can make use of this approach:

Each Step: You can walk slowly and mindfully and with each step repeat one line of the Ho'oponopono mantra.

Problem Solving: Before you set off on your walk think about a problem you would like to solve. This sets you up for your special Ho'oponopono walk; you then proceed to connect to Divinity, through repeating the mantra, and go on a walk and allow the Divine Source to solve the problem for you.

Mala Bead Walk

It can be a nice practice to walk about using mala beads to help you repeat the mantra.

Gratitude Walk

Simply go for a walk in nature and observe all the natural beauty around you. Keep repeating the mantra, *"I love you, "Thank you,"* and allow your feeling of gratitude to expand and radiate outwards.

Relationships

"If you can quickly turn your thoughts to me and to my divine love when you find yourself in a negative situation, everything can change completely. Remember this idea next time. Try it and see how it works." - Eileen Caddy (Opening Doors Within)

Blessing The Person

If you are experiencing a problem or challenge with a certain person give the practice of *Blessing* a go. Think about the person and become aware of any good qualities that they possess, be that character traits, nice hair or clothes, or a pleasant sounding voice tonality. You now begin to bless those good qualities by repeating the mantra: *"I love you. Thank you."* You can also practice this silently in the persons presence - it will help you re-focus your mind away from critical thoughts towards positive appreciation.

The Blessing Circle

This is a nice exercise to start your day off before going to work. Think about all the people you will be interacting with during the day, both the people you get along with and those not so well, and then write each of their names on separate little bits of paper (sticky notes work well). Now spread these names around you, in a circle, on the floor and being to practice blessing these people with the mantra, *"I love you, Thank you,"* while slowly turning around the circle. Do this for a few minutes until you start feeling more warm and open hearted.

*Note: As a variation of this method you could place names of all the people you know into a hat or jar, and then pick a name out at random to practice blessing on.

Relationship Shadows Into De-Light

The following method was inspired by, *"The 3-2-1 Shadow Process,"* (Integral Life Practice) and NLP techniques such as those described in my previous book, *"The NLP Toolbox."* Going through the steps below enables you to bring your own shadow aspects to light, transmute them with Ho'oponopono, while developing more empathy and compassion for yourself and the other person. You may well be surprised and delighted at what's revealed with the following method, so give it a go now:

Relationship Shadows Into De-Light

It's best to do this exercise standing up, allowing yourself to physically move location when you are switching into a different Perceptual Position. (Time required: 15/20 minutes.)

1. 1st Position (Associated or Self Perspective)

Notice the person you are having a challenge with in front of you. Describe the qualities that cause you feelings of aversion or attraction. You can let go and express your feelings fully and completely.

2. Imagine talking to this person in front of you, as if they were really there. Express what it is that bothers you about them, such as, *"you are sooo sexy, you are driving me crazy!"* or, *"you are controlling and domineering!"*

Now begin to ask them questions and listen to their responses:

- *"Why are you doing this to me?"*
- *"What do you want from me?"*
- *"What are you trying to show me?"*
- *"What do you have to teach me?"*

Thank them for their feedback.

Notice how you are feeling and ask yourself, *"what do I need to let go of within myself?"* Now practice Ho'oponopono for a few minutes.

3. 2nd Position (Other Person Perspective)

Before switching into 2nd Position, first of all, ask the person in front of you permission to *step into them*. If you get a positive response go ahead and step into their *perceptual position*, otherwise you can just imagine standing next to them instead, looking over their shoulder at yourself.

Stepping In: Imagine stepping into the other person's shoes, becoming them; see through their eyes, hear through their ears, think their thoughts and feel their feelings. Of course from this perspective you will be looking back at yourself. Now, as this person, begin to embody the qualities you identified in Step 1 of this process; e.g.) They annoy you or they drive you crazy with their sexiness. Use *"I statements,"* so you say things such as, *"I drive people crazy with my sexiness,"* or,

"I am really good at annoying people." Allow yourself to notice how this feels to embody these qualities.

As this person, looking back at *yourself*, answer the question, *"what does that person need to let go of?"*

Remaining in this Perceptual Position, practice Ho'oponopono for a few minutes.

4. 3rd Position (Disassociated Perspective, Neutral or Meta Position)

So you can see the two of you *"over there."* From this perspective what new insights can you make about the relationship dynamic? You could ask yourself, *"what can I learn from this relationship dynamic?"*

Notice how you are feeling and ask yourself, *"what do I need to let go of within myself?"* Now practice Ho'oponopono for a few minutes.

5. 1st Position (Associated or Self Perspective)

Step back into 1st Position, looking at the person in front of you, and notice any new insights or learnings and ask yourself, *"What is it that I need to let go of within myself?"*

Now practice Ho'oponopono, sitting down if you prefer, for at least 5 minutes; 10 minutes is better.

Top Tip 1: If you feel the need you can repeat the steps going through the Perceptual Positions as many times as you like.

Top Tip 2: As soon as possible meet up with the person, in real life, and notice how things have changed in your perception of the relationship dynamics.

Top Tip 3: Practice this method regularly, making use of a Diary to help you keep on keeping on, so that you will continue enhancing your capacity to love yourself and others more authentically.

Obsessive Thoughts

Sometimes in our relationships with others we suffer from obsessive thoughts about the other person. These could be negative critical thoughts or obsessive infatuated thoughts if you find the person really attractive. A useful analogy is that are thought patterns are like the patterns in a groove of a vinyl record. When we are suffering from obsessive thoughts it's as if the record has a scratch in it and the same pattern keeps getting repeated again and again, until we take the needle off the record.

Ho'oponopono enables us to *take the needle off the record* and get back in tune with our authentic loving self. So, with practice, anytime you find yourself slipping into an obsessive groove you can start repeating the Ho'oponopono mantra and re-connect with the source of unconditional love.

Aka Cords And Our Energetic Connections

The term *aka cords* comes from the Hawaiian mystical traditions. It's used to describe the invisible energetic connections between all objects in the Universe. We have aka cords connecting us to objects such as car keys, coffee mugs and with living beings such as our pets, and of course people. The people we interact with a lot, and especially our loved ones, have many aka cord connections with us. So if you are having a challenge with someone you can utilise the knowledge of aka cords to clear the negative *charge* that is being triggered between you both:

1. Think about the person you are experiencing a challenge with. Imagine they are stood in front of you.

2. Notice your feelings. Where in your body do you feel an energetic connection with that other person.

3. And you can imagine energetic aka cords emanating from these parts of your body to the other person's body.

4. Imagine, in whatever way works best for you, the aka cord connection between your own and the other person's Higher Self or Soul; maybe you sense this as a golden thread connection between a glowing orb of love energy above your own head and the other persons.

5. Now, keeping with this visualisation, start repeating the Ho'oponopono mantra for a few minutes.

Ideal Partner Manifestation

If you would like help from the Universe to find your ideal partner give the following method a go. It utilises the power of Blessing, combined with the energetic aka cord connections we have with other people.

1. Begin by thinking about your favourite attributes in an ideal partner, including body features and personality qualities. You can say to yourself, *"I would like to be with someone that is..."*

2. Imagine this amazing person is stood in front of you. You can visualise them in all their beauty or just get a sense of their energy.

3. Now notice your feelings as you connect with this ideal partner. Remember they exist somewhere in the Universe and they are waiting to meet you!

4. Allow yourself to become aware of the aka cord connections you have with this other person; which parts of your body connect to the other person via aka cords?

5. Now being to repeat the Blessing mantra (*"I love you, "Thank you"*) towards this special person for several minutes.

After doing this exercise, maintain awareness for synchronistic signs that could lead to you meeting your ideal partner.

Money & Finances

Money Magic Ho'oponopono

For this exercise grab some notes out of your wallet/purse. If you have a more uncommon note such as a £50 or £100 note, even better. Now hold some of these notes in your hand and begin to practice Ho'oponopono for a few minutes. Next grab a few copper coins and practice Ho'oponopono.

Doing this exercise regularly everyday will help you clear negative associations you have with money and specifically cash. You can do more *clearing work* with your money associations by doing the same exercise with bills, receipts, bank and credit card statements.

Problem People

According to Ho'oponopono all of our problems arise because of *data* stored in our subconscious minds. So if you are having problems with your bank manager, a problematic business partner, clients, or business services etc., it's useful to keep in mind the idea that we are all interconnected and that we share *erroneous data* with others. We don't really know what the problem is, it could be ancestral memories for example, but we can take Total Responsibility and *clean the data*. Think about one of your *problem people* and then being to repeat the Ho'oponopono mantra for, say, ten minutes. Repeat if needed and remember that you are surrendering to Divinity to solve the problem for you, so you can relax and let go.

Poverty Thinking to Prosperity Thinking

The modern world can be really stressful, especially in the area of money because it has such an influence on day-to-day living. When we get overwhelmed with bills to pay, debts, money owed us, car maintenance etc., we can slip into a state of *poverty thinking*; a fear based mind-set of lack. This state of fear can cause a lot of misery and the person's awareness for effective problem solving and openness to opportunity becomes limited.

To shift the thinking patterns from lack to abundance requires you cultivating a state of gratitude or thankfulness for what good things you already have in your life. And there is always much more than you first realise! So being to think about all the wonderful things you have in your life; a house, a car, a dog, a hi-fi, a computer, your partner, your children, your family, your friends, your garden, your health and so on.

Now as you think about each item one-by-one, being to repeat the following Blessing mantra again and again; *"I love you," "Thank you."* Do this exercise everyday and you will discover more and more things to be grateful for. Cultivating gratitude will help you develop an abundance mind-set and it allows inspiration to come through.

Bless Wealthy People

Sometimes we become critical of people that are richer or more affluent than ourselves. Envy is a form of resentment, a negative state of mind caused by erroneous *data* in our subconscious. We can do Ho'oponopono on our feelings of envy to purify that *data* or we can take another approach, which is to Bless the rich person. To do this we contemplate their good qualities, such as; nice clothes, nice car, lovely big house, their businesses provide jobs for people, financial intelligence, good discipline and so on. And then you proceed to Bless them by repeating the following mantra again and again: *"I love you," "Thank you."*

A Taxing Problem

Many people suffer with stress and anxiety when dealing with governmental Tax collection agencies. If you are having problems with a Tax issue it's always worth giving Ho'oponopono a go. Remember, we don't really know what is happening in reality and that our interconnectedness with other people (i.e. people that work at the Tax office) involves shared *data* in our collective subconscious mind. So it's always worth *cleaning* on this *data* to help solve our problems: Think about your Tax problem, the people involved or just get a sense of them in the Tax office, and then proceed to do Ho'oponopono for a few minutes. Do this practice everyday for a week if necessary and see what results you get from it.

Health & Wellbeing

Ho'oponopono Walks

One of the simplest, purest forms of exercise you can do is to go for a walk. So a wonderful thing to do is combine walking with Ho'oponopono practice. Think about a problem you would like to solve, start doing Ho'oponopono, and then go for a walk, repeating the mantra as you enjoy walking along in the fresh air.

Body Healing

From the Ho'oponopono perspective, all of our ailments, including illness and body pain, is due to erroneous *data* stored in our subconscious. So if you are experiencing pain in part of your body, you can practice Ho'oponopono healing by gently touching that part of your body, or just think about it, while reciting the mantra. Practice this every day to help soothe your symptoms. You can also use the same method for skin rashes, wounds or sores.

One of the interesting things about illness or health problems is that it could be a way for your body to communicate with you. Could it be possible that your skin rash is indicating that you need to let go of, *"your irritation with so-and-so?"* You can actually sit quietly and ask the ailment directly, *"What is it you're trying to teach me?"*, or, *"What are you showing me that I need to let go of?"*

Ho'oponopono Fragrance

The effects of beautiful fragrances and perfumes on one's consciousness is well known, and incense has been used for centuries in meditation and healing sanctuaries. So a very simple yet wonderful thing to do to enhance your Ho'oponopono practice is to select a new fragrance that you can use to scent the room when you are reciting the mantra. You can try using different incense sticks, chips, cones, woods, essential oils, or candles. The unique aroma will become associated with your practice and ultimately, your authentic loving self.

The Art Of Blessing

Modern day people have developed very critical minds. We are really good at finding fault with things. Put another way, we could say we are good at cursing things! This attitude doesn't lead to happiness and the antidote is to practice blessing things: You observe a beautiful bird on a tree and you repeat the following phrase again and again like a mantra: *"Thank you", "I love you."* Essentially *blessing* is an exercise that helps you see the good in all things and it cultivates gratitude.

You can practice Blessing on anything you want from looking at yourself in the mirror, to blessing the tiny little birds singing on the trees. Other things you can Bless include:

- Your food at meals times before you eat
- The water that flows from the tap
- Problem people
- The sunshine / the rain

- Your house
- The bus / the train / the tram
- The stars

One of the best things you can do, which is an alternative to *problem solving Ho'oponopono walks*, is to go for a *Ho'oponopono Blessing walk*; you simply stroll along, noticing the incredible nature surrounding you, while repeating the Blessing mantra; *"I love you," "Thank you."*

Take The Needle Off Depression

From the Ho'oponopono perspective, depression is caused by erroneous subconscious memories or *data* arising from the subconscious mind. There are different levels of depression but with effort and persistence you can rise up out of states of depression and cultivate more happiness.

A useful analogy is to think about depression as being like a broken record: the depressing thoughts keep looping around, as if the needle is stuck in the groove. Practicing Ho'oponopono is analogous to picking up the needle and placing us back onto a mellifluous groove.

Daily Practice to Lift Depression

- Keep the Ho'oponopono Principles on your pillowcase, contemplate them, and then repeat the Ho'oponopono mantra every day before going to sleep. Do the same ritual on arising in the mornings.

- 5 Minutes of Mirror Work: Look at yourself in the mirror everyday while repeating the mantra.

- Blessing Walks: Walking is highly recommended for lifting depression. Make it even more potent by practicing the Blessing mantra (*"I love you, "Thank you."*) while taking a stroll.

- Think about other people that are in living in much worse conditions than you (watch the news if necessary) and then practice Ho'oponopono on the feelings (*data*) that it provokes inside yourself.

- Remember your authentic loving self as often as possible throughout each day. You can use stickers or notes around your house to help you remember.

Other Cool Tools

Alpha Brainwave Mantra Trance

You can do this exercise sitting or standing but it's best done outdoors where you've got an expanse to look at. Simply begin by staring off into the distance and move your eye's slightly upwards, approximately 20 degrees (this activates relaxing Alpha brainwaves). Hold this position with a soft gaze and allow yourself to go into a bit of a trance state as you being to recite the Ho'oponopono mantra.

Decision Making

Many people struggle making decisions from time to time, especially important life changing decisions. Unfortunately most of our thoughts are based on *data* arising from the subconscious *database* which influences our decision making process. The method Dr. Hew Len uses with big decisions is to clean on it three times. So, as an example, let's say you were deciding whether or not to invest in a business: You would do three separate Ho'oponopono *cleaning* sessions on that decision and then notice what inspiration and clarity transpires, enabling you to make the best choice.

Ho'oponopono Language

If English isn't your native language try practicing Ho'oponopono in your mother tongue, or any other language you prefer, and discover how it changes your experience.

Ho'oponopono Reminders

It's very good idea to create some little *Ho'oponopono Reminders* because life get's busy and we can get easily distracted. The simplest thing to do is to use sticky notes or just pieces of paper and write, *"Ho'oponopono,"* or, *"Ho'op,"* and then place them around the house, office, car and so on. If you have some artistic talent you could create beautiful sigils or symbol reminders. And if you prefer you could use special physical objects, such as gem stones, as reminders too. The benefit of placing *Reminders* is that when you see one of them it will prompt you to start repeating the mantra; the idea is to be practicing Ho'oponopono as much as possible.

Ho'oponopono Eraser

It can be fun to use a pencil with an eraser on the end to help you *clean on things*. You start by writing your problem down (or the name of a problem person) on a piece of paper and them tap or rub it with the eraser while repeating the Ho'oponpono mantra. You can also use this method to tap or rub on bills.

Top Tip: Get yourself one of those really chunky pencil's with a big eraser on the end.

Wrathful Ho'oponopono!

If you are feeling really angry, for whatever reason, you can begin repeating the Ho'oponopono mantra in an angry tone, either out loud or just inside your mind. It can actually feel really good to allow yourself to repeat the phrases in an angry tonality. See how long you can angrily do it before your state of mind starts to change… You might even start laughing!

Ho'oponopono Magic In A Bottle

Here's a wonderful thing to do! Write down the Ho'oponopono mantra on a piece of paper: *"I love you." "I'm sorry." "Please forgive me." "Thank you."* Decorate it with beautiful patterns or flowers if you have the artistic skill and then place the note inside a glass bottle with a cork or screw on top. Then take a trip to the beach and toss the *message in a bottle* into the ocean when the tide is going out. Practice Blessing *("I love you, "Thank you.")* as you watch the magical bottle float out into the ocean knowing that a random stranger is going to be blessed by this special gift.

Appendix

The 4 Stages of Awakening

The following is a simple model of the stages of awakening we go through as a human being, taken from Joe Vitale's book, *"At Zero: The Final Secrets to Zero Limits"*

1. Victimhood: This first stage is where most people live. No matter what is happening, it is everyone else's fault or at least someone else's fault. It's the world of the blame game. This is where most people live, as Thoreau pointed out, *"lives of quiet desperation."*

2. Empowerment: *The Secret, The Attractor Factor*, and *Think and Grow Rich* are all about empowerment. It's where you can intend, visualize, and manifest. It's fun - even thrilling. But at some point you run into something you have no control over, often a death or serious illness, and you are faced with limitations. You realize you don't control it all. You can't. This prepares you for the next stage.

3. Surrender: This third stage is the stage of Ho'oponopono as Dr. Hew Len taught it to me. You don't try to run the world. You strive to release your intentions and allow inspirations. You trust a process that is already at work. You learn to tune in to an undercurrent from the Divine. You trust it.

4. Awakening: In this final stage, your ego merges with the Divine mind. Almost nobody gets here, but some do. From the outside, you can't say who is enlightened or not. There's no way for you to know. And it comes by grace. You can't make awakening or enlightenment happen. It's not up to you.

All you can do is clean, clear, and prepare. Again, the Law of Attraction isn't dismissed any more than grade school would be to a college student. It's part of your evolution. It's part of the ladder of awakening or, as the late Dr. David Hawkins might have put it, the map of human consciousness. They don't conflict. They are simply on different planes of spirituality.

"I wish you peace beyond all understanding."

Further Reading

If you want to discover more about Ho'oponopono and how you can solve life's problems, while deepening your connection with your authentic loving self, you will probably enjoy reading my book, *"Love Yourself Lovable: Realising Your Authentic Loving Self Through The Profound Yet Simple Practice Of Ho'oponopono."* Claim your copy on Amazon in Paperback or Kindle version by searching for: B01N6QUDYY

Websites

http://zero-wise.com

http://www.self-i-dentity-through-hooponopono.com

http://www.morrnahsprayer.com

http://www.mabelkatz.com